The World of Dogs

A Fully Illustrated Guide to Man's Best Friend

The World of Dogs

A Fully Illustrated Guide to Man's Best Friend

Rebecca King

GRAMERCY BOOKS
NEW YORK

This 1999 edition is published by Gramercy Books™,
a division of Random House Value Publishing, Inc.,
201 East 50th Street, New York, New York, 10022.
by arrangement with PRC Publishing Ltd, London.

Gramercy Books™ and design are registered trademarks of
Random House Value Publishing, Inc.
Random House
New York • Toronto • London • Sydney • Auckland
http://www.randomhouse.com/

Printed and bound in China
A CIP catalogue record for this book is available from the Library of Congress.

ISBN 0-517-16128-1

8 7 6 5 4 3 2 1

Photo Credits:
Animal Photography (Sally Anne Thompson) for Front Cover and Back Cover and pages 2, 6, 7, 9, 22, 23, 25, 26,
27, 28, 30, 31, 32, 33, 35, 36, 37, 38, 39, 40, 41, 42, 43, 44, 45, 46, 47, 48, 49, 50, 51, 52, 53, 54, 55, 56, 57, 58
(both), 59, 60, 61, 62, 63, 65, 66, 68, 69, 70, 71, 72, 73, 75, 76, 77, 79, 80, 81, 84, 85, 87, 89, 90, 91, 92, 94, 95,
96 (bottom), 97, 100, 101, 102, 103, 104, 105, 106, 107, 109, 110, 111, 115, 116, 117, 118, 119, 120, 121, 122,
123, 124, 125;
Angela Hampton/RSPCA PHOTOLIBRARY for page 10, 98, 99;
E A Janes/RSPCA PHOTOLIBRARY for pages 11, 21;
Alan Robinson/RSPCA PHOTOLIBRARY for pages 12, 13, 15;
Duncan I McEwan/RSPCA PHOTOLIBRARY for page 17;
Colin Seddon/RSPCA PHOTOLIBRARY for pages 18, 19;
Roger G Howard/RSPCA PHOTOLIBRARY for page 20;
Animal Photography (R Willbie) for pages 24, 29, 34, 64, 67, 74, 78, 82,
83, 86, 88, 93, 96 (top), 108, 112(both), 113, 114.

Contents

Introduction

Right and Below: The "Sheltie" was originally bred on the Shetland Islands off Scotland's north coast and makes an excellent watchdog — a good example of the relationship that has developed between humans and dogs.

The origins of the domestic dog are obscure, but it is now generally accepted that the 350 or so recognized breeds in existence today are probably all descended from the Grey Wolf (*Canis lupus*), a species of the genus *Canis*, which is a member of the Canidae family. All wild dogs, jackals, coyotes, and foxes (35 species in all) are also members of this family, grouped into 13 genera. They are spread all over the world. In zoological terms, all domestic dog breeds are classed as one species, *Canis familiaris*; and there are more variations in this species than any other, wild or domestic.

The wolf, thought to have been in existence for about 300,000 years, was once one of the most widely distributed mammals in the northern hemisphere, inhabiting a diverse range of habitats. It is believed that there would have been individual varieties that differed in size and color, and gradually these differences became more pronounced and regionalized. In the north, the wolf tended to be large with a thick, pale-colored coat, while in the south it was smaller with a short, darker-colored coat. It is these variations that paved the way for the evolution and development of the domestic dog in all its forms, and were the basis for the many colors and types of coat seen in today's breeds.

Man's association with dogs goes back many thousands of years. Scavenging wolves were sometimes tolerated because they warned tribes of approaching danger from other wild animals. Later, stray cubs were taken in and tamed. Analysis of fossils around the world, however, suggests that real domestication of the dog took place between 10,000 and 15,000 years ago, and evolved primarily because it became evident that wolves and semi-wild dogs could help man hunt for food. This was due to a combination of factors that included dogs' predatory instincts as carnivores, their social nature, and their acceptance of a pack "leader," be it man or wolf, which meant they could be trained. In some parts of the world, dogs may also have been domesticated so that they could be killed and used as food themselves.

By Roman times, recognizable types of dog (notably the Greyhound, the Mastiff, and the northern Spitz breeds that are still clearly identifiable as a "family" today) had evolved as a result of breeding programs and natural selection. Later, their co-existence with man had progressed to such a degree that there were strong fighting dogs, hunting dogs of all sorts, large dogs with thick coats used for protecting herds of sheep in cold, mountainous areas, guard dogs, tracking dogs, herding dogs, sled-hauling dogs, sporting dogs, and water dogs; there were even companion dogs.

Over the next few hundred years, varieties within these broad types became increasingly specialized, and the dog's relationship with man grew more closely entwined: dogs were represented in art; they had religious significance; they appeared in court; they performed in circuses; and they were used in sports. As laws, fashions, and ways of life changed and developed, so too did the dog. Selective breeding became an increasingly precise science; dogs were bred for whatever task man fancied, and were kept by every sector of society.

Despite these very clear differences between types, however, dogs were not actually classified as specific breeds until the mid-19th century, when the concept of the dog show evolved and the need for well-defined physical criteria against which individual dogs could be judged was highlighted. This need led to the formation of the Kennel Club (KC) in Great Britain in 1873, which set ideal standards for each breed ("breed standards") and resulted in stud books being kept. The American Kennel Club (AKC) was formed in 1884, and later similar organizations were established in other countries. These include Europe's Federation Cynologique Internationale (FCI).

With the establishment of these ruling bodies, the fashion for dog shows and the quest to produce the best possible example of a given breed really took hold. The world's most famous dog show, Cruft's, founded by Charles Cruft, was first held in 1890. It began as a show for Terriers only, but soon included other breeds, and enjoyed the patronage of Queen Victoria.

Today, a number of breeds that no longer have a working role in society are finding recognition in the showring and, as a result, gaining international popularity. Many breeds hitherto known only in their country of origin appeared in the United States and elsewhere this century; some have been saved from extinction as a result.

For purposes of classification, all breeds registered by the Kennel Clubs are placed into groups based on the different purposes for which dogs have been bred over the centuries. In the United States, the groups are Sporting, Hound, Working, Terrier, Toy, Non-Sporting, and Herding. The Herding Group was established by the AKC in 1983, because it decided that the Working Group (in which the herders were included) was too large, both in terms of numbers of breeds and numbers of dogs. In Britain, the Working Group still includes the herding breeds, the Non-Sporting Group is called the Utility Group, and the Sporting Group is called the Gun Dog Group.

About 150 breeds are registered with the American Kennel Club and about 190 with the British Kennel Club. There is some variation between the two clubs into which groups certain breeds are placed, as well slight differences in some breed names.

As a result of the two organizations developing independently, breed standards differ slightly between the American and British Kennel Clubs, and, to complicate matters further, from time to time changes and refinements are made to the breed standards of each country. Laws also differ with regard to the cropping of ears and the docking of tails, the former practice being illegal in Britain.

Choosing a Breed

With such a range on offer, choosing which particular breed of dog to keep as a pet is not as straightforward as it might first seem, and a number of factors need to be taken into consideration. It is all too easy to be attracted by the look of a dog without paying due regard to its temperament or day-to-day needs. What is certain is that there is a dog to suit almost any situation or person. All breeds have different strengths and weaknesses, according to preference, and the trick is to select one that matches your requirements and expectations. There are many more breeds in existence than is commonly known, and it is worth researching them all to find a dog that will really suit you. Never forget that the ancestry of a breed and the purpose for which it was bred is fundamental to its character, and these general traits should be studied. Hounds, for example, are often difficult to train and, once let off the leash, unwilling to return until they are ready to do so. Terriers can be hard to keep in a confined space, and love to dig up the garden.

Having chosen a breed, talk to breeders and owners who can offer first-hand experience of the dog in question. One of the prime considerations is how much time you have to spend on your dog. Long-haired breeds requiring daily grooming; energetic dogs needing a long walk off the leash everyday; dogs that need training and patient discipline; dogs that dislike being left alone—these all demand serious commitment on the part of the owner.

Breed behavior and temperament are also very important and must be compatible with your household and way of life. Many small dogs, for example, are not particularly tolerant of young children; large dogs, in general, need plenty of space (although the amount of exercise required is not always directly proportional to size); some breeds have a tendency to

Favorites on both sides of the Atlantic, Golden and Labrador Retrievers (Golden Retriever seen below) make ideal family pets, as do English Springer Spaniels (Right). However, when choosing a sporting dog such as these, remember that they will need a lot of exercise.

bark more than others, which can become trying in certain circumstances; others can be intolerant of strangers; some make better companions than others; certain breeds are essentially working dogs and do not take well to an idle life, and so on.

Long-term expense is another factor. Certain breeds are more prone to diseases and thus run a higher risk of incurring veterinarian's bills, and, of course, large dogs cost more to feed.

Finally, there remains the question of whether to buy a dog or a bitch. With a bitch, there is the inconvenience of her coming into season twice a year for about 20 days and the risk of her producing an unwanted litter. She will also need to be kept away from male dogs (not always easy) and would-be suitors may be a nuisance. If not required for breeding, a bitch should be spayed. Male dogs, on the other hand, can be more aggressive (depending on the breed), especially with other dogs, and may be easily distracted and made restless by the scent of a bitch in season. Neutering will make a dog less restless and less prone to wandering and chasing, but it will not necessarily make him less aggressive if that is his nature. In general, bitches tend to make better family pets, although male dogs, once trained, can be very responsive and devoted companions. Both make equally good guard dogs.

Buying a Puppy

Assuming that you have chosen to buy a pedigree dog, the first step is to do some research into the local breeders. Veterinary surgeries may be able to supply a list of breeders in the area, as can the American Kennel Club. A reputable breeder is the ideal place from which to buy a puppy. Pedigree puppies are also available from pet stores in the United States, but you will not be able to see the parents to assess the likely temperament of the puppy.

The price of a pure-bred puppy will depend upon its pedigree and its popularity to rarity ratio. Dogs intended for showing will be more expensive than those to be kept as pets only, and you will probably have to wait a few months before you can take the puppy home, by which time its show potential will be established.

The next step is to visit one or two kennels, not only to talk to the breeders but also to see how the dogs are kept. Having then decided upon a breeder, make arrangements to see the litter with its dam to select your puppy. This will normally be when it is about four weeks old. Known inherited breed defects should be discussed, and the temperament of the dam—and that of the sire too, if possible—should be assessed.

Make sure the puppy you take to (or the one that takes to you) is healthy and lively. Watch it running around and playing. It is never a good idea to pick the runt of the litter, or the one cowering in the corner, because you feel sorry for it. Check that the skin feels soft and fairly loose, that there is no trace of fleas in the coat, and that there are no signs of diarrhoea. Note that a very distended belly may indicate an infestation of worms. Examine the puppy's eyes, nose, and the insides of its ears for signs of discharge or soreness.

Having selected a puppy, arrange with the breeder when to take it home. This is usually when it is between eight and ten weeks old, by which time it should have been fully weaned and wormed at least once. Within a day or two of collecting your new puppy, take it to a veterinarian for a full check-up and to plan a program of inoculations.

Right and Below: Always choose a healthy and lively puppy and examine it carefully before buying. Once you have colected the dog, take it to a veterinarian for a check-up. This is a Jack Russell puppy.

Preparing the House and Yard

A young puppy can cause a lot of damage or harm itself in a house or yard that has not been adequately prepared for its arrival. Remember that for a while it will be scooting around the house, jumping on the furniture and tugging at the edges of tablecloths. First of all, remove from harm's way anything that might easily get broken or knocked over, and check for chewable items such as electrical wires and cables. Secondly, make sure any chemical cleaning materials or garden preparations are inaccessible. Outside, preventing the puppy from escaping from the yard is the first priority. This will mean fencing the entire perimeter—up to about 4 feet (1.2 metres) high for a small dog and 6 feet (1.8 metres) for larger dogs—of your property, making sure that it is well secured at the bottom. Any gaps in hedges should be blocked with wire netting. Some dogs, particularly Terriers, will try and dig their way out under fencing. Front and back gates must be easily and securely fastened, and make sure that there isn't a large enough gap at the bottom for the puppy to wriggle under.

An alternative to fencing the yard is to build an enclosed pen, ensuring that it is large enough for the breed in question to be able to play and run around in.

Dog Care

Keeping a dog, whatever the breed, takes time, money, and commitment. A puppy can be quite hard work, especially during the first few weeks, so be sure to take this into account when buying it, and plan holidays and other events accordingly. The key is to establish a sensible routine from day one and to stick to it. When the puppy first comes home, care should be taken not to overwhelm it with fuss and attention. Let it explore in its own good time, and introduce it to new people and situations gradually. Don't leave it alone for long periods, and if there are other pets in the house watch them carefully with the new arrival for a good week or so.

Bedding

Puppies sleep a good deal of the time, and it is important that they have their own warm, safe bed. There are many types of bed on the market, but make sure that the one you choose is draught-proof, can be cleaned easily, and is big enough to accommodate the fully grown dog. To start with a stout box is a good bet as it doesn't matter if it gets chewed. Bedding should be soft, warm, and washable.

The bed should be placed somewhere draught-free and quiet, but it

As soon as the puppy is brought home, introduce it to its bed and make sure it sleeps in it from the word go. Letting it spend the first few nights tucked up in bed with you may seem an easy option, but you will live to regret it. In the early days, a securely wrapped hotwater bottle and a ticking clock may comfort it when you leave it for the night. Harden yourself to pathetic whimperings, but never scold a puppy for making them.

Puppies do a lot of sleeping and—as these Spaniels show—are very happy to do so companionably.

Feeding

The breeder should have provided you with a feeding program for your puppy, and possibly some of the food it is used to. It is wise to stick to this for the first few days at least, and introduce any change of diet gradually so as to avoid stomach upsets. Clean, fresh water should be available to the puppy at all times. Designate a set of suitable, flat-bottomed feeding and drinking bowls for the puppy's sole use. Preferably, these should be ceramic or stainless steel; plastic bowls may be chewed or played with, and are easily knocked over. They also tend to skid around the floor as the puppy tries to eat. Long-eared breeds need a deep bowl to keep their ears out of the food.

As a rough rule of thumb, puppies up to the age of four months require four meals a day, from three to six months three meals, and from six months to a year two meals. Most adult dogs are happy with one meal daily, although very small breeds (and a few large breeds given to bloating) may be better with two or even three smaller meals. Care should be taken not to overfeed breeds that run to fat easily (notably Spaniels and Retrievers), or are particularly greedy. An overweight dog will be less active, and prone to heart and back problems. Remember that as dogs age they require less food.

Toys

Playing and chewing are an important part of a puppy's development and it is important to provide it with its own supply of safe, specially designed toys—there is a huge range on the market. Keep items that you don't want to become playthings well out of its way. Discarded children's toys are not usually suitable. Avoid any small items that the puppy may be able to swallow whole.

Chewing also helps to keep an adult dog's teeth and gums healthy, so appropriate toys should be available to it at all times.

Grooming

The amount of grooming a dog requires varies according to its coat type. All breeds need some grooming, however, to stimulate the skin and keep the coat in a healthy condition. There are a number of different brushes and combs available to suit the job in hand; be sure to get the right ones. It is advisable to get a young puppy used to grooming as soon as possible so it can quickly and easily be trained to stand quietly, preferably on a box or table for ease. Having to groom a long-haired dog that thinks the whole procedure is a game (or a battle) is a nightmare, and the result will be that grooming doesn't happen nearly often enough.

Smooth-haired dogs require no more than a quick brush over a couple of times a week with a soft bristle brush or a rubber brush, although during periods of moult—usually in spring and fall, each lasting four to six weeks—it is best to brush daily if they shed a lot of hair.

Many long-haired breeds, on the other hand, need quite specialized, time-consuming care that mustn't be underestimated. The coats of the Old English Sheepdog, Yorkshire Terrier or Great Pyrenees, for example, need to be groomed for up to an hour daily otherwise they will quickly become dirty, smelly, and matted and the hair will have to be cut off or even shaved.

Some wire-haired breeds, as well as being brushed regularly, need to have their coats stripped once or twice a year, which involves pulling out the old hair by hand or with a stripping knife to allow the new hair to grow through. This is best left to a professional. Do not be tempted to have a dog such as this clipped instead (a cheaper option) as this does not allow the skin to breath in the same way and may lead to skin problems.

Poodles have to be brushed and clipped regularly as their coat just grows and grows and can become matted if neglected; they have the advantage, though, of not moulting. Any breed with a dense, woolly undercoat must be kept free of mats at all cost.

If necessary, delicate areas such as around the eyes and ears can be gently trimmed with blunt-ended scissors, but *never* cut the muzzle whiskers. Keep hair that grows between the toes well trimmed.

Regular checks should be made of your dog's ears, particularly if it is a long-eared breed. Wiping the inside of the ears with surgical spirit will help to prevent problems. Check your dog regularly for sores, rashes, or lumps. Teeth, too, should be examined from time to time, and if there is a buildup of tartar, take the dog to a veterinarian so they can be scraped. If your dog shows a sudden unwillingness to eat, or develops bad breath, more often than not a problem with its teeth or gums is the cause.

A dog's nails need to be kept clipped (special clippers can be bought) and this can usually be done at home. Ask your veterinarian to give you a demonstration. Take great care not to cut too close to the nail bed, or it will bleed.

It is only really necessary to bathe a short-haired dog when it has rolled in something smelly. Use warm water and a special medicated shampoo, rather than household detergents that can cause skin problems. Some long-haired breeds will require bathing more often to keep their coats in prime condition, but this should never be excessive as it will destroy the coat's natural water-proofing qualities. Dry shampoos are often a good alternative.

Exercise

All dogs require regular exercise of some sort to keep them happy and healthy, but the amount and type obviously varies greatly from breed to breed. Beware of over-exercising very large breeds up to about the age of 18 months, as this can put undue stress on their bones and cause lasting damage. Playing games is a good form of exercise for many breeds, and during these sessions a dog can be trained to fetch and drop an object on command.

A puppy should be introduced to the collar and leash quite early on in life, so it is not frightened by them and can be gradually trained to walk quietly at heel without pulling. This is particularly important with large or strong dogs, as it is essential that by the time they are full-size whoever is exercising them has control, and not the other way around. An adjustable leather collar with a name tag attached is probably the best bet for a young puppy. Make sure it is neither too tight nor loose enough for the puppy to slip out of. On older, stronger dogs, choke chains (properly used) are an effective way to train a dog, but they should not be left on all the time.

Remember that puppies should not be walked on the streets or allowed near other dogs until their first course of vaccinations is complete, usually at about 14 weeks.

Left: If you live by the sea, exercising dogs is usually straightforward.

Training

This covers many aspects of your dog's behavior and makes the difference between a dog that is a pleasure to own and one that is a nuisance, or even a danger. The amount of training a dog needs depends largely on the breed in question and what you intend to use it for, and this should be carefully considered as not everyone has the time, physical capability, or disposition to train a strong, independently-minded animal.

All dogs should walk to heel, come when called, and stay, sit, or lie down on command, and this basic training can be integrated into everyday life from about the age of three to four months. More advanced obedience training does not normally start before about eight months. Any specific training sessions should be kept to between 10 and 20 minutes in length, be fun, and be concluded on a high note. Generally, it is better for one person to take on the training of a dog.

Right and Below: The golden rules when training a dog are consistency, repetition, firmness, and lavish praise—and patience is prerequisite!

The golden rules when training a dog are consistency, repetition, firmness, and lavish praise. Remember that dogs, having evolved from wolves, are pack animals by nature and expect to have leader. Once an owner is recognized as such, therefore, a dog will instinctively be receptive to orders from him or her. Dogs cannot learn by reasoning, however; they simply associate actions and rewards with doing something right or wrong. Never give mixed messages to your dog, or try and do more than one thing at a time—it will become confused and unresponsive. If a dog repeatedly fails to do what is being asked of it, you are probably not being clear enough.

The tone of your voice is all-important: sound as if you mean it when you are scolding your dog, without resorting to shouting, and inject genuine pleasure into your voice when it has done something right. Rewards for good behavior are important, but food rewards, although invaluable, should only be given every now and again. Praise and a pat should be enough most of the time. Commands issued in association with hand signals are effective in the early stages.

There is rarely a need for physical punishment when training a puppy, but sometimes a firm shake or a light slap on the rump is called for. Praise or punishment must always be immediate (within a few seconds). Punishment long after the "crime" is useless as your puppy will think it is being punished for what it did 10 seconds ago and start to mistrust you.

House training

House training is usually the first priority and should begin as soon as you bring your puppy home. The trick is to predict the calls of nature by taking the puppy outside to the same place whenever it wakes, about 15 minutes after eating, after exercise, after any period of two or so hours during which it has not urinated, or at any sign of restlessness or circling. Never punish your puppy when there is an accident (there will be many),

but rather give lavish praise when it performs in the right place. Paper-training is a good interim measure if you cannot be with the puppy all day or live in an apartment. Where accidents do occur, use a strong disinfectant to deter the puppy from using the same place again.

Traveling in a car

It is important to train you puppy to lie quietly in the car as an animal likely to jump on the driver's knee is obviously very dangerous. Introduce the car to your puppy when it is stationary, and begin by taking it on very short trips, gradually building up to longer journeys. Use either a small cage or a dog guard until you can be sure of your dog's behavior. It is a good idea to combine a trip with a walk, then the dog will look forward to going out in the car. Never leave a puppy (or adult dog, for that matter) alone in the car without making sure it cannot come to any harm and has sufficient ventilation, particularly in hot weather.

Below: Dogs should lie quietly in the car, which must always be well-ventilated. Pets can overheat and dehydrate very quickly if left in a sealed car. Here, a well-behaved Golden Retriever makes himself comfortable.

Bad habits

Ideally, these shouldn't be allowed to start in the first place. Bad habits—such as expecting to be fed tidbits from the table, jumping up at people, jumping on furniture, or barking excessively and inappropriately—are all hard to break and should be firmly nipped in the bud. When an adorable puppy does these things it might seem not to matter, but don't think that the puppy will grow out of such habits, or that you can easily correct them later, as this is not the case.

Dog Breeds

Hound Group

The domestication of dogs stemmed from their usefulness to man in hunting for food, and hounds (a distinct group of hunting dog) were therefore one of the first types of dogs to be bred. Featuring among the earliest documentation of dogs are the Greyhound and the Afghan Hound, which were established in the Middle East at least 5,000 years ago.

Hounds can be broadly divided into two groups: sight hounds and scent hounds. Sight hounds, also known as gaze hounds or long dogs, hunt silently by sight and are epitomized by the Greyhound. Typically long-legged, lightly-built and fast, with good lung capacity, they were capable of giving chase to and running down large, swift animals, such as deer and wolves, over open terrain. They tend to have a roach back, sloping down toward the tail, and the head is long, with the eyes positioned prominently to give a good range of vision. There are both long-coated and short-coated breeds.

Scent hounds, typically smooth-coated with pendulous ears, sniff out prey and put it up for the chase. European in origin, they were developed much later than sight hounds, and are heavily built and possess great stamina. The head shape is quite different to that of a sight hound, ending in a square muzzle that allows room for wide nasal passages. Their hindquarters are strong, enabling them to plough through undergrowth after their quarry—rabbits, badgers, and foxes. Scent hounds usually hunt in packs in woodland, and to keep in contact with each other and the huntsmen have deep, baying calls that carry over considerable distances. Their upright sterns (tails) help them to be seen in the undergrowth. In general, they are tricolored (black, white, and tan) or bicolored (black and white or tan and white). Some breeds of hound have been named after the animal they are intended to hunt.

In the United States, scent hounds are far more popular than sight hounds, perhaps because, in general, the former are more sociable and tolerant of other dogs than the latter, and lack the killer instinct possessed by some sight hounds. All hounds are easily distracted by sights and scents, and are not always easy to discipline. As a group they require a lot of exercise.

Right and Below: The Beagle is the oldest of the British hounds with a documented history stretching back over 500 years.

Afghan Hound

This aristocratic, elegant creature is thought to have originated in Egypt and then became established in Afghanistan where it was used by the nobility to hunt hare, deer, gazelles, and wolves. It is referred to as the "king of dogs." As a coursing hound, the Afghan hunts by sight and is extremely fast and agile. Its instinct to chase and kill is still very strong, which, together with its independent nature, means a very firm hand is required. The very long, silky coat can be of any color.

Basenji

The Basenji, which was not exported until the 1930s, came from Central Africa where it was used to hunt vermin and small game. One of the most curious features of this friendly little dog is that it emits a yodeling-like sound instead of a bark. The breed's wrinkled forehead, tightly-curled tail lying over the back, and tireless, swinging gait are also characteristic. It has a short coat that can be chestnut, or black with white markings, or tricolor.

Right: Basenji.

Basset Hound

The Basset has one of the finest noses of the scent hounds and can hunt game such as hare, rabbits, and pheasant tirelessly, albeit slowly, for long periods. The Basset group came from France and is known to date back to the 17th century at least. The name may have come from the French word *bas*, meaning "low." As well as its very short legs and long ears, which give it a rather comical appearance, the Basset is distinguished by its deep, baying voice. The short coat is tricolor or lemon and white.

Above: Basset Hound.

Beagle

Traditionally, the Beagle has been used to hunt hare, accompanied on foot, but it has become highly popular as a pet and makes a delightful companion. Affectionate and friendly as it is, however, the Beagle is not renowned for its obedience and requires a fair amount of exercise for its size. It also does not like to be left alone for long periods. This is one of the oldest of the British hounds, with a documented history stretching back 500 years or so. It has a short tricolor or lemon and white coat.

Bloodhound

First and foremost the Bloodhound is a tracker dog, although it will not attack its quarry and is not in the least aggressive. Its ancestor was the St. Hubert Hound, an ancient European breed favored by royalty. Surprisingly sensitive—given its great size—the Bloodhound can be rather reserved with a solemnity that is reflected in its expression. This is a greedy dog by nature and should be fed little and often to avoid stomach problems. The short coat is colored black and tan, liver and tan, or red.

Right: Beagle.

Below: Bloodhound.

Borzoi

Like the Afghan, the Borzoi is an aristocratic sight hound that can run at great speed. From the 13th century it was kept by the Russian nobility to course hare or hunt wolves—they often worked in pairs to bring the wolf to the ground. Plenty of space and exercise is required for this dog, and it is not always easy to train. The long, silky coat can be curly, wavy, or flat, with a thickly feathered tail. The color is not specified.

Dachshund

Originally bred in Germany to kill badgers in their setts, the Dachshund (often referred to as a "sausage dog" because of it elongated body on short legs) has become one of the most popular family pets in the United States. There are six varieties—long-haired, smooth-haired, and wire-haired, with a standard and miniature version of each. Each breed has its own heritage and characteristics, but all Dachshunds are lively and make good watchdogs and companions; they have a surprisingly loud bark.

Right: Borzois.

Below: Standard Smooth-haired Dachshunds.

Irish Wolfhound

This lays claim to being the largest (in terms of height) breed of dog in existence, and has a fine, ancient pedigree as the hunting dog of Irish royalty. However, with the extinction of its chief quarry (wolves) in the 18th century, the breed's popularity declined and would have disappeared altogether had it not been for the efforts of one Captain Graham who resurrected it by careful crossing with the Deerhound. Rough-coated and of variable color, the Wolfhound is a gentle, affectionate dog.

Norwegian Elkhound

Right: Norwegian Elkhound.

Below: Irish Wolfhound.

A member of the handsome Spitz family, the Elkhound, in some form, has been in existence for several centuries. It was first used in northern Scandinavia to hunt elk and other large animals, such as moose, wolves, and bears. It has an amazing sense of smell. Devoted to its owner, the Elkhound is a good watchdog and loves the outdoor life, although it does not need an inordinate amount of exercise. Despite its dense coat the Elkhound can tolerate heat—unlike some other Spitz breeds.

Rhodesian Ridgeback

Named for the ridge of raised hair along its spine, which grows in the opposite direction to the rest of its coat, the handsome Rhodesian Ridgeback is in fact a South African dog thought to have descended from the semi-wild Hottentot hunting dog. Strong and fearless with great stamina, it was used to hunt lions. The Ridgeback makes an excellent watchdog and a good companion, but requires dedicated training if it is to be kept inside the house.

Saluki

Known as the "Gazelle Hound" in Britain, the Saluki is as fleet and grace-ful as its namesake, which it hunted. Another of the sight hounds originating in the Middle East, it is one of the contenders for "oldest known breed of domestic dog" and was much prized by Arab and Persian nobility. Highly intelligent and undoubtedly extremely elegant, the Saluki is a sensitive dog that requires gentle handling and lots of exercise. The soft, silky coat and long hair on the ears are characteristic. Any color is acceptable.

Right: Rhodesian Ridgebacks.

Below: Saluki.

Right and Below: Whippets.

Whippet

The Whippet, a descendant of the Greyhound, is the smallest of the sight hounds and one of the easiest dogs to keep as a pet. It is gentle and obedient, clean and undemanding. It was developed in the 19th century in the north of England primarily as a racing dog, but it was also used for catching rabbits. Although introduced to the United States at the beginning of the 20th century, it was not recognized by the American Kennel Club until 1976. Due to its fine coat (which can be any color), the Whippet tends to feel the cold.

Sporting Group

Whereas hounds were developed to hunt and sometimes kill animals, initially out of a need for man to obtain food, sporting dogs were developed to help man to hunt game, including birds, purely for pleasure. Different breeds evolved (mainly in North America and Britain) for the specific purposes of locating and stalking game, flushing it out of cover, and retrieving it from the undergrowth or water. With the invention of firearms, a whole new dimension was added to the sport of hunting, and the types of sporting dogs, or gun dogs as they are known in Britain, increased.

The first sporting dogs to appear on the scene were Pointers, which locate game by scent and then freeze with their noses pointing in the direction of the prey. Originally, the startled quarry was then coursed by sight hounds or captured by falcons. Next came the families of Spaniels and Setters, both derived from the Old English Water Spaniel. These dogs flushed out the game so it could be killed, and then retrieved the dead bodies. A third group, the Retrievers, was bred specifically to collect the dead bird or animal, often from water, and bring it back to its master undamaged. Those dogs that can do this well are known to have a "soft mouth" and are much sought after. Retrievers are the most gentle and placid of the sporting dogs, unequalled for temperament and reliability. In Europe, sporting dogs have been bred more as all-rounders, rather than for specific tasks.

Characteristics common to the group include a willingness to please, a good nature, intelligence, and a tendency to be quiet. This makes them very likeable pets, although most breeds are still used in the field as well. All sporting dogs require off the leash exercise in open country, and thrive on human company. Many have soft, wavy coats and are particularly handsome.

Right and Below: Labrador Retriever.

Brittany
Formerly known as the Brittany Spaniel, this French sporting dog combines the attributes of a Retriever with that of a Pointer. In appearance it has more the look of a Setter than a Spaniel, hence its change of name. Introduced in the 1930s, the Brittany is one of the most popular sporting breeds in the United States, but its adaptable and responsive nature, plus the fact that it is easy to train, makes it a good household pet as long as it has the freedom and stimulus of the open countryside.

Chesapeake Bay Retriever
This breed is native to the shores of Chesapeake Bay and, as a wildfowl retriever, is as home in the water as it is on land. The Chesapeake is a strong, robust dog. Its thick, slightly oily outer coat and dense, woolly undercoat enables him to hunt in all conditions and plunge into icy lakes or rivers. The color of the coat, usually referred to as "dead grass," is important as camouflage. This is definitely an outdoor dog that likes to work.

Right: Brittany.

Below: Chesapeake Bay Retriever.

Cocker Spaniel

Derived from its larger English counterpart, which was introduced to the United States at the end of the 19th century, the American Cocker Spaniel became a separate breed in the 1930s, recognized by both the British and American Kennel Clubs. The hair on its legs and underbelly reaches to the ground and requires diligent grooming daily. The Cocker makes a good family pet, being friendly and easy to train. It comes in a wide variety of colors.

English Cocker Spaniel

Right: English Cocker Spaniel.

Below: Comparison between the English Springer Spaniel (two at left) and American Cocker Spaniel (on the right).

This is the forebear of the American Cocker Spaniel, more than likely named because of its ability to flush out game, woodcock (considered a delicacy) in particular. It is also a good retriever. Cockers are busy, very affectionate dogs, always eager to please and seemingly always in high spirits. The English Cocker is much easier to keep groomed than its American counterpart, although its long ears need looking after. It likes a lot of exercise, but adapts well to being kept solely as a pet.

English Setter

Like most sporting dogs, the English Setter is intelligent, keen to please, and makes a loyal and affectionate companion. However, as a breed it needs open countryside in which to race off its energy and high spirits, and a firm hand to keep it under control. The English Setter has all the streamlined elegance of others of its kind, with a silky, wavy coat and heavy feathering. It comes in a variety of flecked colors, referred to as belton, that are always mixed with white.

English Springer Spaniel

Nearly all Spaniels have evolved from the large, handsome Springer. It was developed in the Middle Ages specifically to spring (flush) the game from the undergrowth for falconers, hence the name. Today, it is also used to retrieve. Like most sporting breeds, its superb temperament and devotion to its owner make the Springer a delightful pet, especially if children are around. This is a boisterous breed, though, that needs a fair amount of off the leash exercise. Liver and white or black and white are the preferred colors.

Right: English Springer Spaniel.

Below: English Setter.

Right: Flat-coated Retriever.

Far Right: German Short-haired Pointer.

Flat-coated Retriever

Lighter in build and more racy than other Retrievers—reflecting the fact that it was probably bred from Setters, Spaniels, and the Newfoundland—the Flat-coated Retriever makes an intelligent and devoted pet. It thrives on human company and, apart from needing regular country walks, is little trouble to keep. The flat, glossy coat is commonly black, but it can also be liver-colored; the coat is fine and dense with feathering on the legs and belly.

German Short-haired Pointer

There are three distinct breeds of German Pointer—long-haired, wire-haired, and short-haired—of which the short-haired is the most common. Descended from the Spanish Pointer, English Foxhound, Bloodhound, and German Tracking Hound, this is generally considered to be one of the best all-round sporting dogs. Leggy and clean-cut with a short coat, the German Pointer can be liver, black, liver and white, or black and white. It needs to lead an active life if it is to be kept as a pet.

Below: Golden Retriver mother and puppies.

Golden Retriever

This is a very gentle, extremely handsome breed that is prized both as a sporting dog (for its soft mouth and obedience) and as a household pet (for its good nature). Although it is easy to train and makes an excellent companion, the Retriever needs to be kept occupied and likes to be around people. Like the Labrador, this is a greedy dog and can run to fat easily if not exercised regularly. The thick, wavy coat can be any shade of yellow from cream to deep gold.

Gordon Setter

Developed in Scotland in the 17th century by the 4th Duke of Richmond **Above: Gordon Setter.**
and Gordon, this is the largest and heaviest member of the Setter family,
all of which are very handsome dogs. The Gordon has great stamina
when out in the field, where it excels at locating game, but, being somewhat calmer in temperament than other Setters, also makes a gentle and
dignified companion when kept in the right environment. Its coloring is
black and tan only.

Irish Setter

This very beautiful, deep red-colored dog (also known as the Red Setter) was bred in Ireland from various other Setters, Pointers, and Spaniels as a bird dog. Originally red and white, the pure red form emerged in the 19th century and subsequently became extremely popular. Rather less biddable than most other sporting breeds, the Irish Setter is quite highly strung. It needs a huge amount of vigorous exercise and gentle but firm discipline, as it has boundless energy and high spirits.

Labrador Retriever

The near perfect temperament of the Labrador is its greatest asset and goes some way to explaining its supreme popularity as a family pet, far outstripping other breeds. This good nature, combined with intelligence and reliability, also makes it a superb guide dog for the blind. The Labrador originated in Newfoundland, where it helped fishermen drag their nets through the sea, and the breed is still a great lover of water. The thick, coarse coat is virtually waterproof, and the chunky tail, which is used like a rudder, is known as an "otter tail." Colors are black or yellow, and, less commonly, liver.

Right: Irish Setters.

Below: Three colors of Labrador Retriever—black, yellow, and liver.

Right and Below: Pointer.

Pointer

Before guns were used in sport, the Pointer was used to find the game (usually hare) and "point" to it so the Greyhound could then give chase. Later they were used to locate other game, which could then be shot. This lean, handsome breed is a descendant of the much heavier Spanish pointing dog that dates back to the Middle Ages. Although essentially an outdoor creature, the Pointer will give devoted service to an active master. A variety of colors from solid to tricolor is acceptable.

Vizsla
Sometimes known as the Hungarian Pointer, this is the national dog of Hungary (and the country's only shooting dog). The Vizsla is an excellent all-rounder in the hunting field, being able to point, flush, and retrieve from both land and water. It looks similar to the Weimaraner, from which it is probably in part descended. Lean and athletic, the Vizsla has tremendous energy and stamina and needs to be kept well exercised to prevent it getting bored. Its name means "responsive and alert."

Weimaraner
This sleek, clean-limbed dog is noted above all for its unusual silvery-gray color and light amber or blue eyes. Perfected as a breed in Germany during the 19th century, it first left the country in the late 1920s to be bred in the United States. It is essentially a water retriever and is noted for its soft mouth. The Weimaraner is not quite as easy-going as other sporting breeds, and requires careful training and a good deal of exercise. It can be quite protective of property and therefore makes a good guard.

Right: Weimaraner.

Below: Vizsla.

Terrier Group

Terriers have their roots firmly in Britain, as their names (such as Cairn, Yorkshire, Manchester, and West Highland) suggest. They have been in existence since Roman times, but the majority of breeds seen today were developed in the late 18th and 19th centuries to seek out (burrowing underground if necessary) and kill small animals that were regarded as pests—rodents and rabbits in particular. As a result they are tenacious and brave, ready to take on all comers. Terriers were also used by huntsmen to tackle the fox in its earth after it had been run to ground by the hounds. The word Terrier comes from the Latin word *terra*, meaning "earth."

These were tough, working dogs, largely restricted to the area in which they were bred. Some breeds remain relatively localized, whereas others—such as the diminutive Yorkshire Terrier (now categorized as a Toy breed)—have become internationally popular and can be found far from their native regions. As well as hunting, Terriers were used for sports such as ratcatching, which became very popular with the working classes of Industrial Britain in the 19th century.

Many Terriers, bred to work outside, have coarse, wiry coats that require regular stripping (see page 16), but there are also a number of smooth-coated breeds. On the whole, the breeds in this group are small- to medium-sized, the largest member being the long-legged Airedale Terrier from Yorkshire.

Despite their small size Terriers are not lap dogs, as their hunting and fighting instincts remain strong and they have boundless energy. They make lively, entertaining pets of real character, but often tend to be one-man dogs and are not particularly sociable with other animals. They are also quite vocal and love to dig holes or ferret out something that has caught their interest. All Terriers need quite a lot of exercise and play to prevent them from becoming bored.

Confusingly, not all breeds with the name Terrier are categorized in the Terrier group—some appear in the Toy and Working groups.

Airedale Terrier

Nicknamed "king of Terriers," the Airedale was first bred in the mid-19th century in the north of England to hunt otters and badgers along the River Aire. Its ancestors are believed to be the Black and Tan Terrier (see Manchester Terrier) and the Otterhound. Later, it was used by the army and police force, a reflection of its intelligence. The Airedale loves water and needs to be well exercised and kept occupied. Although not aggressive, it make a good guard dog.

American Staffordshire Terrier

This breed developed from the Staffordshire Bull Terrier, which was first taken to the United States in the 19th century. In 1972 the prefix "American" was added to differentiate the two, although the breeds had been recognized as distinct since 1936. Originally used to bait bulls, the American Staffordshire is larger and more powerfully built than its cousin across the water. It is an intelligent and strong-minded dog that can become a devoted family pet, but requires careful training and is not good with other dogs.

Below: American Staffordshire Terrier.

Border Terrier

The Border Terrier has all the characteristics typical of the group: hardiness, stamina, tenacity, and intelligence, and it has them in abundance. Bred in the wild Border country between England and Scotland to drive foxes above ground, the breed has changed little in appearance over the years. It is a game, lively, and affectionate dog that requires early training, exercise, and companionship to prevent destructiveness.

Above: Border Terrier.

Bull Terrier

The egg-shaped head is the most distinctive feature of this stocky, powerfully-built breed. Developed for dog fighting and badger baiting, by crossing the Bulldog with the English Terrier in the 19th century, its aggression toward other dogs remains a strong feature of its character. That said, however, as far as its owner is concerned, it is a gentle and loyal dog. There is a tendency to deafness in all-white Bull Terriers. In Britain, the white Bull Terrier and the colored Bull Terrier count as one variety.

Right: Wire-coated Fox Terrier.

Far Right: Cairn Terrier.

Below: Smooth-coated Fox Terrier.

Cairn Terrier

One of the oldest breeds in the Terrier Group, the Cairn originated in the Scottish Highlands. It is named after the piles of stones, known as cairns, that dot the landscape. Fearless and full of fun, the Cairn likes to make its presence felt and can be noisy. This breed does not require a great deal of exercise, but the shaggy outer coat and dense, soft under-fur need regular brushing.

Fox Terrier

There are two varieties of Fox Terrier, wire-coated and smooth-coated, each recognized as a separate breed. The wire-coated is the most popular as a pet and showdog. Apart from their coats, however, the two breeds are identical, and were originally bred for hunting both above and below ground. Firm early training to control their strong hunting instincts makes them lively and devoted pets, but they do need a lot of exercise. The wire-coated variety needs stripping twice and year.

Kerry Blue Terrier

The Kerry Blue takes its name from the region in southwest Ireland in which it originated and the color of its soft, wavy coat. The puppies are born with a black coat that does not change color for about 18 months. It does not molt, but must be kept well brushed and needs to be trimmed regularly. Self-possessed and friendly, the Kerry Blue makes a lively pet and a good watchdog, but it is not always keen on the company of other dogs.

Manchester Terrier

This is one of the few smooth-coated Terriers and is more streamlined than most, indicating its Whippet blood. Developed in Manchester, England, during the 16th century to excel in the two sports of rabbit hunting and ratcatching, it has replaced the Black and Tan Terrier from which it evolved. Clean, companionable, good-natured, and undemanding in all respects, the Manchester Terrier makes a very good all-round family pet. It is always glossy black with tan markings.

Right: Kerry Blue Terrier.

Far Right: Manchester Terrier.

Miniature Schnauzer
Classified outside the United States and Canada as a working dog, the Miniature Schnauzer is the smallest member of the Schnauzer family (and the most popular in the States, where it has been bred since 1925) that originated in Germany as cattle-dogs and ratcatchers. It is an affectionate and lively little dog, though it can be wary of strangers. The wiry coat needs to be brushed regularly and clipped to keep a neat appearance. Its characteristic long whiskers gave rise to its name, which means "muzzle."

Scottish Terrier
Known as the 'Scottie," this appealing, solid little Terrier was originally called the Aberdeen Terrier, as that was where the breed was first developed to hunt foxes after they had gone to ground. Although very affectionate and companionable, the Scottie has a mind of its own and needs to be trained well as a puppy. Its wiry coat should be trimmed about twice a year and the long whiskers washed from time to time.

Right: Miniature Schnauzer.

Below: Scottish Terrier.

Soft-coated Wheaten Terrier
Popular in the United States, although not found widely elsewhere, the Wheaten Terrier originally came from Ireland in the 18th century, where it was kept on farms to guard, herd, and keep down vermin and other pests. Its lovely soft, pale-colored coat (the color of ripening wheat, never reddish) doesn't molt, but needs to be kept free of tangles and trimmed occasionally. Good natured and high spirited, the Wheaten is an entertaining companion for the active owner. The tail is usually docked.

Staffordshire Bull Terrier

Right: Staffordshire Bull Terrier.

Below: Undocked Soft-coated Wheaten Terriers.

Less popular in the United States than its American counterpart, the pugnacious Staffordshire nevertheless has a loyal following. It developed in Staffordshire, England, as a fighter from a mixture of Terrier breeds and the Bulldog. One of its greatest qualities is its supreme devotion to members of its household, children in particular. As long as it is kept away from other dogs, and its instinct to fight them is curbed at an early age, the Staffordshire makes an undemanding and rewarding household pet.

Welsh Terrier

This is one of the oldest breeds of Terrier. Bred in Wales, it is a descendant of the Black and Tan Terrier (see Manchester Terrier) and was greatly favored as a working dog. Intelligent and easy-going, the Welsh Terrier makes an excellent family pet. It is hardy, easy to train, requires only moderate exercise, and will fit into most households. Its upright stance, whiskered square head, and black and tan coloring are similar to the larger Airedale. The wiry coat needs to be stripped professionally.

West Highland White Terrier

A real little character, the "Westie" is full of fun and good spirits. It loves to be at the center of the action and can be very protective of its family. The breed, descended from the Cairn Terrier, is white, possibly so it is easy to spot on the moorland. Only moderate exercise is needed to keep the Westie happy, but it doesn't like to be left alone for too long. Early training will prevent it taking over your life.

Right: Welsh Terrier.

Below: West Highland White Terriers.

Toy Group

In contrast to the breeds in the other groups, most Toy breeds have never had any purpose in life other than to amuse their owners, provide them with companionship and affection, and look decorative. This is certainly their role today, and they fulfill it extremely well.

The tradition began many centuries ago in China, when emperors developed tiny breeds such as the Lion Dog, ancestor of the Pekingese, as companions. This practice later spread to the royal courts of Europe where many miniature dogs were given high status. With the decline of the aristocracy, Toys went out of favor for a while, but came into their own again after World War II as household pets when space—and money—were at a premium.

Toy breeds, despite their size, should never be regarded as playthings; many in fact can be quite demanding and some require a great deal of grooming. They are often very brave, given their size, and make good watchdogs. Any tendency to excessive barking (yapping) should be curbed at an early age.

Their size makes them suitable as town and apartment dogs, or as companions for the elderly who may be unable to give them much exercise, but Toys do require a lot of attention and human company. In return they can be absolutely devoted to (and quite possessive of) their owners. As a rule they are not dogs for households with boisterous children.

Toys need to be fed little and often. Although they do not cost a lot to keep, they can be expensive to buy, as litters tend to be small and there is a high demand for them.

Right and Below: The Papillon, sometimes known as the Squirrel Spaniel, was particularly popular in the 17th century.

Above: Brussels Griffon.

Brussels Griffon
This rather comical-looking, snub-nosed little dog was first bred in the capital of Belgium to hunt vermin. There is a smooth-coated (Petit Brabançon) and a rough-coated variety, which in Europe are separated into different breeds. The latter is the most popular in the United States. This lively little dog is full of character, adaptable, and responsive to training. It has an amusing air of self-importance, yet enjoys a good game. Both varieties come in red, black, and black and tan.

Cavalier King Charles Spaniel
Beloved by royalty, including its namesake, Charles II, the Cavalier King Charles can be seen in many 17th-century paintings. However, the breed of that time all but died out until Roswell Aldridge, a United States citizen, offered financial rewards to breeders in England to produce dogs as near to them in appearance as possible. Gentle, undemanding, and easy to train, the Cavalier is a popular companion to people of all ages.

Chihuahua
This has the distinction of being the smallest dog in the world. Originating in Mexico, it is thought to have descended from the Mexican temple dog worshipped by the Aztecs and was developed in the United States. There are two varieties, long-haired and short-haired, both of which can appear in the same litter. In Britain, the two are divided into separate breeds. Lively, intelligent, and affectionate, the dainty (though sometimes noisy) little Chihuahua becomes very attached to its owner and makes an ideal apartment pet.

Chinese Crested Dog

There are two varieties of this breed, Hairless and the Powder Puff, and both can appear in the same litter. The former is a strange-looking little creature with hair on its head, feet, and tail only. It is allergic to wool and can get sunburnt. The Powder Puff is rather more attractive, with long, soft hair that requires daily grooming. Both varieties crave human companionship and are as happy with a play session as a walk. They should not be overfed.

Italian Greyhound

This smaller version of the Greyhound first gained popularity with the nobility of Italy. Gentle, affectionate, and extremely clean (it has no "doggy" odor), the Italian Greyhound is very easy to keep, but prefers a quiet household and is probably better off without having to contend with the rough and tumble of children. It can feel and catch cold easily.

Left: Chinese Crested Dog.

Below: Japanese Chin.

Japanese Chin

A favorite with royalty and the nobility in Japan for centuries, the Japanese Chin is a delightful little dog that looks like a long-legged Pekingese. Queen Victoria took a fancy to it when it was first introduced to the West, and in 1882 it was taken to the United States. The luxuriant long coat, which comes in black or red with white, requires daily brushing, but this is not a time-consuming job. The Chin has a delightful temperament and requires little exercise.

Maltese

The very long, silky white coat of the Maltese needs to be kept in tip-top condition to do this breed justice, and care must be taken not to expose it to heavy rain or very hot sun. Despite its very ornamental appearance, however, the breed is lively and robust, enjoying both exercise and human company. Generally believed to have come from the Mediterranean island of Malta several hundred years ago, the Maltese was a popular breed with the ladies of the European courts.

Above: Maltese.

Miniature Pinscher
Affectionately known as the Min Pin, the Miniature Pinscher is as bright as a button and very playful. It is quite fearless and makes a good watchdog, but can be a bit nippy. This little dog has a distinctive, high-stepping gait and a great jump, so needs to be kept well fenced in. The familiar black and tan of the Pinscher family is the most common coloring, but the Min Pin comes in a variety of other colors, too.

Papillon
Papillon is the French for "butterfly," and one look at the shape and set of the breed's relatively large, erect ears explains its name. (There is a less common, drop-eared variety, called "Phalène," which means "moth.") Also sometimes known as the Squirrel Spaniel, because of its long bushy tail curled over its back, the Papillon was very popular during the 17th century with the royalty of Europe, and often features in paintings by Old Masters. Lively and intelligent, the dainty Papillon makes an easy companion, although it can become over-possessive of its owner.

Right: Papillons.

Below: Miniature Pinscher.

Pekingese

It is easy to see why these very decorative little dogs were so highly prized by the Chinese Imperial Court, where they were often carried in the sleeves of ladies' dresses or lay on velvet cushions. They first left China in 1860, after the English sacked and looted the Summer Palace in Peking. As well as being beautiful, the Pekingese is intelligent and good natured. Its long, thick coat needs daily brushing, however, and its protruding eyes and squashed nose can give rise to problems. It prefers playtimes to walks as a form of exercise.

Pomeranian

The Pomeranian is the smallest of the Spitz group of dogs, which are all characterized by a foxy face, pricked ears, a tail that curls up over the back, and thick fur. Over the years the breed has got smaller and smaller. Developed in the German province of Pomerania toward the end of the 19th century, it became very popular both in the United States and Britain after Queen Victoria showed an interest in it. Lively, loyal, affectionate, and easy to train, this pretty little dog can be quite vocal and makes a good watchdog. Apart from needing daily grooming, it is very little trouble to keep.

Right: Pomeranian.

Below: Pekingese.

header at top left
78

Below: Pugs.

Pug

This comical-looking, almost ugly little dog is believed to have originated in China and been brought back initially to Holland on the ships of the Dutch East India Company. Solid and compact with a wrinkled face, it is something like a miniature Mastiff. Its novelty value gained the breed great popularity during the 18th century; after a period of decline, it is becoming more widespread. The Pug makes a devoted pet, but needs a lot of attention. Care must be taken with its weight.

Shih Tzu

Like the Pekingese, the very decorative Shih Tzu (pronounced "shidzoo," and meaning "lion") was developed for the pleasure of the Imperial Court of China. Its ancestor was probably the Tibetan Lhasa Apso, which it resembles, and the Tibetan Terrier. The Shih Tzu did not leave China until the 1930s, when it was first brought to Britain (where it is classified in the Utility Group). These little dogs are full of character and fun. The very long coat needs a lot of daily attention.

Above: Shih Tzus.

Silky Terrier

The Silky originated in Australia, where is was bred from various English Terriers, including the similar-looking Yorkshire Terrier. Like the Yorkshire, its long, silky coat requires daily grooming. Surprisingly energetic and lively, the Silky also needs regular exercise and playtimes. In true Terrier fashion, it loves to dig, given the chance, and makes a vociferous watchdog. Its close relative, the Australian Terrier, is categorized as a separate breed in the United States. In Britain, the Silky Terrier is called the Australian Silky Terrier.

Yorkshire Terrier

Right: Yorkshire Terrier.

Below: Silky Terrier.

The most popular member of the Toy Group in both the United States and Britain, the tiny Yorkshire Terrier has a mixed ancestry of various Terriers. The breed, about 100 years old, was originally larger and developed as a ratcatcher. The extremely long, dead-straight hair, customarily tied away from the eyes in a topknot, is generally only seen in its full glory on showdogs as it takes considerable effort to keep well groomed. The Yorkie kept as a pet often has a shaggier, shorter look. It is a lively companion and a good (but noisy) watchdog.

Working Group

This group encompasses an assortment of breeds that have been developed throughout the world for specific jobs of work. On the whole they are large, strong dogs. For centuries the natural territorial instinct of dogs has been exploited and as a result a number of working breeds, such as Great Danes, Dobermans, and Boxers, have traditionally been used to guard property and livestock. In the Middle Ages, packs of ferocious dogs, usually Mastiffs, were kept by the nobility to keep away wolves and other intruders.

Another important role that dogs have fulfilled since early times is one of sled-pulling across snow in northern parts of the world. In Europe dogs have sometimes been used to haul carts or carry loads.

Dogs have also served man through the ages by helping him out of dangerous situations. The Saint Bernard is probably the most famous rescuer and is widely associated with tales of quite amazing endurance and devotion.

All working breeds can be trained very easily, but they have active minds that need to be kept occupied, even if they are no longer being used to fulfill their original role. Some breeds adapt better to being kept simply as pets than others, but all can be loyal and dependable with the right handling.

Right and Below: Doberman Pinscher puppy.

Below: Japanese Akita.

Akita

The Akita, a descendant of the Spitz family, is the national dog of Japan. It was first bred in the province of Akita in the 17th century, where it was used to hunt deer and wild boar. Although intensely loyal and brave, making it an excellent guard, the Akita can be stubborn. It is important to start training early, as it is a powerful breed. Care should also be taken with it around other dogs. It is happy with regular but moderate exercise. The breed is not recognized by the Kennel Club of Great Britain.

Alaskan Malamute

Along with the Siberian Husky, the Malamute closely resembles its ancestor, the Grey Wolf, in appearance. One of the North American Spitz breeds, it was developed by a nomadic tribe called the Mahlemuts to pull sleds and sleighs. It is therefore very strong and has great stamina. Malamutes are friendly and gentle toward people (they don't make good guards), but are not generally good with other dogs. They do not need more than moderate exercise, but do require space. Hot weather does not suit them.

Bernese Mountain Dog

This strong, good-looking dog was bred to pull carts in the Berne canton of Switzerland. One of the four varieties of Swiss mountain dog, it is said to date back to Roman times, when it was used as a guard dog; it certainly makes a good watchdog today. Solidly built, with a thick, silky, wavy coat, the Bernese Mountain Dog has a sound temperament and makes a good family pet—as long as it gets sufficient exercise.

Boxer

Few breeds are as loyal or as protective as the Boxer, a strong dog with lightning reactions, which makes it a good guard. Almost tireless energy and stamina, as well as natural high spirits and great character, are other key characteristics of the breed, and these mean that a lot of exercise and a firm hand are essential. The Boxer as it is known today originated in the 19th century in Germany, where it was used as a police dog.

Bullmastiff

Not recognized as a breed in its own right by the American Kennel Club until 1933, the Bullmastiff was bred from the Bulldog and the Mastiff, and has some of the best qualities of each. It is large, powerful, faithful to its owner and property, and fearless, thus making the breed an excellent guard dog. Despite this it has quite a docile temperament. Surprisingly, given its size, it does not need a great deal of exercise. The short, coarse coat can be red, fawn, or brindle.

Right: Bullmastiff.

Below: Boxer.

Doberman Pinscher
Named after a German tax collector called Louis Dobermann, who developed the breed in the 1870s as a tracking and police dog, the Doberman Pinscher is a streamlined, powerful breed, renowned as a guard dog. The breed's reputation for being fierce and bad-tempered is largely unfounded. Although most commonly black with tan markings, brown, blue, or fawn with tan markings are also acceptable colors. The ears are usually cropped in the United States.

Great Dane
This huge and distinguished-looking dog was kept by German nobility to hunt boars and stags in the Middle Ages. Today, it makes an affectionate pet, but obviously demands a fair amount of space, and is costly to feed. The five recognized colors of the sleek coat are brindle, fawn, blue, black, and harlequin (pure white with black or blue patches). Like the Doberman, the ears of a Great Dane are usually cropped in the United States, but never in Britain.

Right: Great Dane.

Below: Doberman Pinscher.

Great Pyrenees

More commonly known outside North America as the Pyrenean Mountain Dog, this beautiful and very popular "gentle giant" used to guard flocks of sheep in the mountains bordering Spain and France. Though it can be wary of strangers, it has a kindly, docile nature (reflected in its expression) and tends to move at a sedate pace. The very thick, shaggy coat requires considerable grooming; it is mainly white, with patches of grey, badger, or pale yellow around the head.

Mastiff

The Old English Mastiff, one of the oldest breeds of British dog, proved fearless when on the battlefield or pitted against bears and lions in the sporting arena. It all but died out after World War II, but was revived in the United States and is gaining popularity once more. Today's Mastiff is a docile, good-natured dog that needs surprisingly little exercise. It makes a devoted guard dog. Colors are apricot, fawn, silver, or fawn brindle.

Right: Mastiff.

Below: Pyrenean Mountain Dog.

Newfoundland

Above all, this enormous, cuddly, and extremely kindly dog loves the water, and is never happier than when rescuing someone from drowning. It was developed in Newfoundland where it helped save the lives of sailors, but its ancestry is uncertain. The flat, dense, water-resistant coat is black, deep brown, or white with black markings; the last variety is known as the Landseer, after the Victorian English artist Sir Edwin Landseer, who often painted the breed.

Portuguese Water Dog

The Portuguese Water Dog was known in Portugal as long ago as the 16th century, and was used by fishermen to help retrieve lost boats and tackle. Like the Poodle's, its traditional clip was designed to enable it to swim more easily yet keep the internal organs warm in the water; the breed also has webbed feet. The Portuguese has boundless energy, which it must be allowed to use up. If given firm early training it makes a friendly, good-natured companion.

Right: Portuguese Water Dog.

Below: Newfoundland.

Above: Saint Bernard.

Right: Rottweilers.

Rottweiler

The Rottweiler is one of the most popular breeds in the United States. Although it can be aggressive toward intruders, and requires authoritative training by an experienced dog owner and plenty of exercise, it can be an affectionate and obedient member of the right household. Bitches are definitely easier to handle than dogs. The Rottweiler is named after the German town of Rottweil, where the breed's ancestors drove cattle to market and protected them from marauders. It does, of course, make an excellent guard dog. Its sole coloring is black with tan markings.

Saint Bernard

Famous for saving people's lives in the Swiss Alps, the Saint Bernard is named after the Hospice du Grand St. Bernard, which was founded near the Italian border to shelter travelers. The breed—placid and even tempered—has adapted well to domestic life, but it needs a lot of space and is expensive to feed. Prospective owners should also be aware that the Saint Bernard drools a lot. As with any giant breed, early training is necessary if control is to be maintained.

Samoyed

This gorgeous, happy-looking member of the Spitz family was initially bred to haul sleds and herd reindeer in Siberia. Later, fur traders introduced it to Europe and the United States, where it soon found favor due to its

handsome appearance and friendly nature. As well as the spectacular white, the thick coat can be biscuit or cream. Needing only moderate grooming (the outer coat doesn't moult and the woolly undercoat is shed in clumps twice a year) and exercise, this beautiful dog makes a good family pet.

Schnauzer
The Schnauzer family consists of three distinct breeds—Giant, Standard, and Miniature (the latter being classified as a Terrier, see page 62)—and originated in Germany over 500 years ago. The Giant was first used for droving and herding cattle, while the smaller Standard evolved as a rat-catcher. Both solid and square-set, with the characteristic whiskers and harsh, wiry coat, they are loyal and affectionate dogs and make good guards. In Germany and the United States the ears are cropped, but this is illegal in Britain.

Siberian Husky
Developed by the Chukchi tribe in northeast Asia as a means of transport, then taken to Alaska, the Husky's popularity has spread rapidly in the United States. Often it is kept for the sport of sled racing, and this is what it is best suited to. In any circumstances, however, it needs to lead a very active life and be given a great deal of exercise. The Husky is very tolerant of, and affectionate toward, people, but, as a pack animal, can be aggressive with other dogs.

Above: Samoyed.

Right: Siberian Husky.

Below: Standard Schnauzer.

Herding Group

When man began to domesticate sheep, goats, and cattle, the dog came into its own as a herder and protector, and various breeds developed accordingly in different parts of the world.

The early herding dogs tended to be large and powerful, able to protect livestock from fierce predators, such as wolves and bears, and to live out in all weathers. As the predators declined in numbers, however, a number of smaller, more athletic breeds developed for the sole purpose of herding.

Today, each breed is suited to cope with a particular terrain and climate, but all herders, are agile and robust, respond well to training, and show reliability and loyalty. Many also retain a strong instinct to gently round up both humans and animals, and to protect their loved ones.

The decline of their original roles means that these days many herding breeds are kept only for showing or as pets, although field events and sheepdog trials are keeping the traditional working relationship between dog, livestock, and master alive. Some breeds, such as the German Shepherd, have come into their own in quite different areas of work.

When kept as pets, herders are better for being well trained and having a job of work to do; they are not good at being left to their own devices for long.

Right and Below: The Border Collie exemplifies the intelligence and obedience of the herding group.

Australian Cattle Dog

Variously known as the Queensland Heeler, the Australian Heeler, and the Blue Heeler, this breed has been bred specifically to meet the requirements of Australian sheep farmers. The Collie, the Dingo, the Kelpie, and the Dalmatian all figure in the breed's makeup, with the result that it is intelligent, obedient, easy to train, adaptable, and loyal. Sturdy and workmanlike in appearance, with a short, dense coat, this is a relatively easy dog to keep, but needs to be active.

Right: Australian Shepherds.

Below: Australian Cattle Dog and puppies.

Australian Shepherd

It is a bit of mystery as to where the name "Australian" came from, as this breed was developed in the United States in the 19th century. It quite obviously has Collie blood in it and is a prized sheep herder. Like others of its kind, the "Aussie" likes to work and is very intelligent and responsive to commands. Given plenty of exercise, it makes a loyal, good-natured companion. The thick, wavy coat is unusual in that it comes in a multitude of patterns and colors, with no two being exactly the same.

Bearded Collie

The Bearded Collie, an ancient breed traditionally used in the north of England and borders of Scotland for herding sheep and cattle, has enjoyed something of a renaissance in recent years as a pet and showdog in the United States. Between the two world wars it all but died out. Commitment to its grooming and exercise are necessary, but the Bearded Collie makes a lively, fun-loving, and affectionate pet that responds well to training.

Belgian Shepherd Dog

Below: Belgian Shepherd Dog.

There are four different breeds of Belgian Shepherd—Groenendael (known in the United States as the Belgian Sheepdog), Laekenois, Malinois, and Tervuren—each named after the town in Belgium in which it originated. They are mainly differentiated by coat types and color as follows: Groenendael, long black coat; Laekenois, fawn, wiry coat with black face markings; Malinois, smooth-coated, resembling the German Shepherd; Tervuren, similar to the Groenendael apart from the color, which ranges from fawn to dark reddish-brown. All are essentially working dogs requiring a good deal of exercise and training.

Border Collie

The black and white Border Collie (other colors are permissible, but are far less common) originated on the borders of England and Scotland and is one of the most intelligent and easily trained of all sheepdogs. Again and again it excels at sheepdog trials and obedience tests. It is affectionate and loyal as a pet, although with its boundless energy and active mind it needs plenty of stimulation to prevent it from becoming bored. The thick coat can be of varying lengths.

Above: Border Collies.

Bouvier des Flandres

A solid, square-looking dog, the Bouvier was bred from the Belgian Cattle Dog in the 17th century to herd sheep and cattle, but it has become increasingly popular as a non-working dog in the United States. Its rough, coarse coat can protect it against the harshest of weather. Unlike other herding dogs, the Bouvier maneuvers the animal it is shepherding with its body, rather than nipping at its heels. Loyal and brave, it makes a good family pet and is happy with only moderate exercise.

Briard

The Briard originated in the Brie district of France several centuries ago as a guard dog, defending both property and livestock. Later, however, it was used primarily to herd sheep. The breed has only recently become widely known outside France—it was first taken to the United States after World War I. Like other long-haired Collies, the Briard has to be groomed daily. It makes a loyal, lively, and intelligent companion to those prepared to give it the exercise it needs.

Canaan Dog

The Canaan, a descendant of the pariah dogs of the Middle East, has been guarding livestock in the deserts of Israel for thousands of years. This is an athletic dog, alert and responsive to training, but it needs a lot of exercise. True to its past history, it is a good watchdog and wary of strangers. Colors range from red to sandy-yellow, or black and white.

Right: Canaan Dog.

Below: Briard.

Cardigan Welsh Corgi

Distinguished from the Pembroke Corgi by its slightly longer body, larger ears, and long bushy tail, giving it a foxy appearance, the Cardigan is one of the oldest British breeds. It is a tough little dog bred to herd cattle, which it did by nipping at the animals' heels then dodging smartly out the way. The two Corgi breeds have only been classified separately for about 75 years. The Cardigan tends to require more exercise than the Pembroke, but is otherwise undemanding. It is not, however, especially good with children.

Collie

In the United States the rough and smooth varieties of the Collie are judged by the same standard, apart from reference to their coat, whereas in Britain they are granted separate status. The rough variety is by far the most popular due to its very handsome appearance, and has gained worldwide recognition through the *Lassie* films. Originally bred (like all Collies) in Scotland to herd sheep, the Rough Collie has been more of a showdog and pet in recent years. It is friendly and intelligent, although it can be wary of strangers.

Below: Cardigan Welsh Corgi.

German Shepherd Dog

Highly valued as a guard dog, police dog, and guide dog, the German Shepherd is also a popular pet in the United States. It was introduced to Britain and the United States from Germany (where it was developed as a herder) by soldiers returning home from World War I. Strength, courage, and intelligence are its key qualities, and, once trained, the German Shepherd can work without direction or instruction. The breed requires regular exercise and training, however, and needs to work. Any color apart from white is acceptable.

Above: German Shepherds.

Above: Pembroke Welsh Corgi puppies.

Right: Old English Sheepdog.

Old English Sheepdog

This is a very time-consuming dog to keep as its shaggy coat needs a great deal of grooming. It also needs a lot of training and exercise. Nicknamed the "Bobtail" because the tail is traditionally docked, it came from the southwest of England in the 19th century, where it was used as a herding and droving dog. The Old English Sheepdog makes a good guard dog and a loveable, if boisterous, family pet. Its rolling gait is very distinctive. Any hint of brown in the coloring is not acceptable.

Pembroke Welsh Corgi

Of the two Welsh Corgis, Pembroke and Cardigan, the former is by far the most widespread in the United States. It is known for its popularity with Queen Elizabeth II. The Pembroke is a very old breed, believed to have been used for droving cattle in Wales as long ago as the 11th century. It is commonly red and white, but comes in other colors too. The Pembroke is easy to keep as a pet, but its tendency to nip should be curbed at an early age.

Right: Smooth Collie.

Below: Rough Collie (behind) and Shetland Sheepdog.

Shetland Sheepdog

The "Sheltie," with its dense coat, magnificent mane, and appealing expression, is a very attractive little dog that resembles the larger Rough Collie. Originally known as the Shetland Collie, the breed was developed on the Shetland Isles off the north coast of Scotland. It is intelligent and easy to train, and makes both a good watchdog and a good companion, although regular grooming is required. It comes in a wide variety of colors.

Non-Sporting Group

This group is a somewhat disparate bunch, consisting of breeds that do not readily fit into any of the other six groups; they are sometimes referred to as "companion" dogs, as that is now their main function.

What the members of this group do have in common, however, is that either they weren't bred to fulfill any particular working requirements in the first place, or their original role no longer exists. As a result, any strong fighting, hunting, or territorial instincts have been bred out of them over the years, making them affectionate and tolerant toward humans and animals alike, with no overriding drives. In addition, their energy and stamina levels tend to be moderate, as they have no inherent need to keep active for long periods of time—there are obvious exceptions to this, such as the Dalmatian.

Although non-sporting breeds are all quite different in appearance and nature, they share the charm of possessing a lively, individual character, intelligence, and very distinctive looks. In general, they are small to medium sized.

Far Right: The Keeshond was originally kept on barges in Holland. As with so many of the original functions of the dogs in the Non-Sporting Group, that original use has become less important over the years. Today, the Keeshond is known as a watchdog.

Right: Boston Terrier.

Bichon Frisé

There is some dispute over the origins of this charming, fun-loving little dog, but it may have been taken to the Continent from the Canary Islands in about the 14th century. During the 16th and 17th centuries it enjoyed great favor in the royal courts of Europe, but during the 19th century it was more widely seen as a circus turn. In this century, it has gained great popularity in the United States. The white, fluffy, curly (*frisé* is French for "curly") coat of the Bichon takes a good deal of daily care.

Boston Terrier

Like the Tibetan Terrier, the Boston is a Terrier in name only, which it gains from its ancestry. It was bred in the 19th century in the United States from the British Bulldog and the White English Terrier. Later, French Bulldog blood was introduced. Very intelligent, undemanding in terms of grooming and exercise, and with great character, the Boston is understandably a very popular pet. It is both good with children and an effective watchdog. Colors are brindle or black, both with white markings.

Below: Bichon Frisé.

Bulldog

Despite its history as a fighting dog, principally used for the sport of bull-baiting, the present day Bulldog is a docile and affectionate breed that is particularly good with children. With its huge head, squashed-in face, and thickset body reflecting its Mastiff ancestry, no-one would call the Bulldog a handsome dog, but this most British of breeds is hugely popular in the United States. The Bulldog requires only moderate exercise, and is very prone to heat stress.

Above: Bulldogs.

Chinese Shar-pei

In the middle of this century the Shar-pei was in danger of extinction, but after being re-established in the United States it is now among the top 40 most popular breeds. It came from China, where it was bred for dog-fighting—its extraordinary loose, wrinkled skin was developed so it could wriggle away from an adversary with ease. Skin infections and an abnormality of the eyelids have to be reckoned with in this now amiable breed.

Right: Chow Chow.

Far Right: Dalmatian.

Chow Chow
The furry, lion-like Chow Chow was first bred in China over 2,000 years ago, and during its history it has been used as a guard dog, to pull carts, as a hunting dog, and as a source of food and fur. Known only in the West since the late 19th century, it is now a prized showdog. Although it can be affectionate, the Chow Chow has an uncertain temperament, can be jealous of its owner, and is not good with other dogs. It comes in a range of solid colors. Like the Shar-pei, the Chow Chow has a blue-black tongue.

Dalmatian
The unmistakable Dalmatian is traditionally known as a carriage dog; it was also used to accompany horse-drawn firewagons in the United States. This clean-limbed, handsome breed has great stamina and requires strenuous exercise. Although high-spirited, it is excellent with children and loves playing with them. Training needs to be gentle and firm. As well as the familiar black-spotted variety, there is a liver-spotted version. The puppies of both are born pure white.

French Bulldog

The ancestry of this sturdy little dog is obscure, but it is thought to have been bred in the 19th century from a small variety of the Bulldog, which was taken to France and then to the United States. Here the breed was developed with the characteristic large, upright ears. The French Bulldog is inclined to be greedy and can easily run to fat, but otherwise makes a playful and undemanding pet. Care should be taken that it does not overexert itself in hot weather.

Keeshond

Originating from Holland, where it was traditionally kept on the barges as a companion, ratcatcher, and guard, the hardy, silvery-gray Keeshond has all the characteristics of the Spitz breeds: a thick coat with a magnificent ruff, pricked ears, and a tightly curled tail. It does not require a great deal of exercise, but loves company and needs to be groomed daily. It also benefits from early training as it can be independent. The Keeshond is a good, but noisy, watchdog with a distinctive, ringing bark.

Right: French Bulldog.

Below: Keeshond.

Lhasa Apso
This is another of the ancient breeds from Tibet that reached the West this century and has subsequently become enormously popular. Sometimes difficult to tell one end from the other due to its long, profuse coat, it needs diligent daily grooming, but otherwise is little trouble to keep. Favored colors are gold and cream, but others are possible. The Lhasa Apso is intelligent, affectionate, and easy to train, making it a delightful addition to any household. It also has excellent hearing, which means it is a good watchdog.

Poodle
Originally bred in the 13th century to retrieve waterfowl, the Poodle comes in three sizes: Standard, Miniature, and Toy (placed in the Toy Group). Few breeds are as intelligent as the Poodle—its responsiveness to training and natural sense of fun gave rise to its success as a circus performer in the 19th century. The coat, which does not moult, has to be clipped every six weeks or so, but otherwise the Poodle is an undemanding and rewarding pet to keep, although it must have plenty of human company.

Right: Standard Poodles.

Below: Lhasa Apso.

Schipperke

A small member of the attractive Spitz family, the Schipperke (pro-nounced "skipperkey") was originally used as a guard dog on barges in Belgium. Solid black is the only color acceptable to the United States stan-dard, but elsewhere other solid colors are permissible. Unlike other Spitzs, the Schipperke is usually born tail-less; if a tail is present, it is close-ly docked at birth. Like all guards, the Schipperke is alert and loyal, but can be suspicious of strangers. It is a sociable and affectionate breed.

Shibu Inu

One of the most popular breeds in Japan, the Shibu Inu is being kept increasingly in the United States and elsewhere, although it has not yet caught up with the similar-looking Akita. It is the smallest of the Japanese Spitz breeds, and was first developed to flush out small game from the undergrowth. Although intelligent, friendly, and loyal, the Shibu requires authoritative training. It is an active dog needing a fair amount of exercise. The thick, glossy coat comes in many colors.

Right: Schipperke.

Below: Shibu Inu.

Above: Tibetan Spaniel.

Right: Tibetan Terrier.

Tibetan Spaniel
This breed bears absolutely no resemblance to the Spaniel family either in looks or nature, so its name is a bit of a mystery. It was first bred in the 17th century in the monasteries of Tibet as a companion and watchdog, roles which it fulfills admirably as a pet today. Despite having energy and high spirits, it requires little exercise. The long, silky coat of the Tibetan Spaniel does not need as much grooming as you might expect.

Tibetan Terrier
Despite its name, this is not a true Terrier, as it has never been used to hunt underground. Before it was taken to Britain and then the United States (where it was not recognized for showing until 1973), it had been bred in Tibet for centuries for herding, for use as a guard dog, and as a companion. Its long, shaggy coat needs regular grooming, but otherwise this is a friendly little dog that is gentle and easy to train.

Reference

Dog Magazines

There are many magazines and journals devoted to dogs. Some are listed below but there may be others in your area as well as newsletters from local dog clubs. Most will provide a sample copy before you subscribe so it is worth contacting them if you would like to take a look before you buy.

UK

Kennel Gazette — The Journal of the Kennel Club
The magazine of the Kennel Club has some excellent articles as well as all of the details of the club and upcoming shows.

USA

Dog and Kennel
An excellent bi-monthly magazine that includes regular articles on breed standards, health issues, training, and dog news. They offer a free trial copy on their website, which is at www.dogandkennel.com

Dog World
A great magazine which, like so many, has an equally good website. It features a problem solving service for training and any other questions you might have regarding your dog. www.dogworldmag.com

Dog Registering Organizations

UK

The Kennel Club
1-5 Clarges Street
Piccadilly
London
WIY 8AB
TELEPHONE: 0171 629 5828

USA

American Canine Association
P. O. Box 992, Wilmington, DE 19899,
TELEPHONE: (302) 655-3746
http://www.he.net/aca/index.htm

American Kennel Club
5580 Centerview Drive, Suite 200, Raleigh, NC 27606
www.akc.org

American Rare Breed Association
9921 Frank Tippett Road, Cheltenham, MD 20623
TELEPHONE: (301)868-5718 FAX: (301)868-6409
www.arba.org

Dog Related Internet Sites

There are literally hundreds of web sites dedicated to dogs — breeds, care, shows, and any other information that you could possibly want is on the internet somewhere. If you have ever "surfed" though you will know that the only difficulty can be in locating the right pages! However, it can be fun looking and you might come across some interesting sites along the way. These are some of the best and most offer links to other pages, so they are a good place to start your search.

The Dog Owner's Guide
www.canismajor.com/dog/guide.html

A comprehensive site that has information on breeds, training, grooming, behavior, and health issues.

Dogs On-line
www.dogsonline.co.uk

A great British website which has advertisements from breeders who have puppies for sale.

Digital Dog
www.digitaldog.com

A very friendly site that has a chat forum where you can talk live to other dog lovers. They also have question and answer sessions with the resident trainer as well as special guests.

www.dogzone.com

www.canismajor.com/dog/guide.html

www.dogowners.org

Books on Dogs

American Kennel Club; *The Complete Dog Book*; Howell Book House.

Bruette, Dr. W.A. and Donnelly, K. V.; *Complete Dog Buyer's Guide*; TFH Publications.

Caras, R.; *The Roger Caras Dog Book: The Complete Guide to Every American Kennel Club Breed*; M. Evans and Co. Inc.

Carlson, D. G., DVM, and Giffin, J. M., MD; *The Dog Owner's Home Veterinary Handbook*; Howell Book House.

Caufield, J., and others; *Chicken Soup for the Pet Lover's Soul*; Random House.

Coile, D., PhD; *Encyclopedia of Dog Breeds*; Barrons.

Fawcett, W.E.; *How to Get Your Dog to Do What You Want*; Columbine Books.

Fisher, J.; *Why Does My Dog . . . ?*; Souvenir Press.

Fogle, Dr. B.; *Know Your Dog*; Dorling Kindersley.

Giant Book of the Dog; Chartwell.

Jackson, F. (Ed); *Faithful Friends: Dogs in Life and Literature*; Robinson.

Jackson, F. (Ed); *The Mammoth Book of Dogs*; Robinson.

Kennel Club; The Kennel Club's Illustrated Breed Standards; Ebury Press.

Knott, T.D.; *The Complete Handbook of Dog Training*; Howell Book House.

Milani, M., DVM; *Dogsmart*; Contemporary Books.

Morris, D.; *Dogwatching*; Cape.

Race, D., DVM; *Dogs from A–Z: A Dictionary of Canine Terms*; Barrons.

Taylor, D.; *The Ultimate Dog Book*; Dorling Kindersley.

Taylor, D.; *You and Your Dog*; Dorling Kindersley.